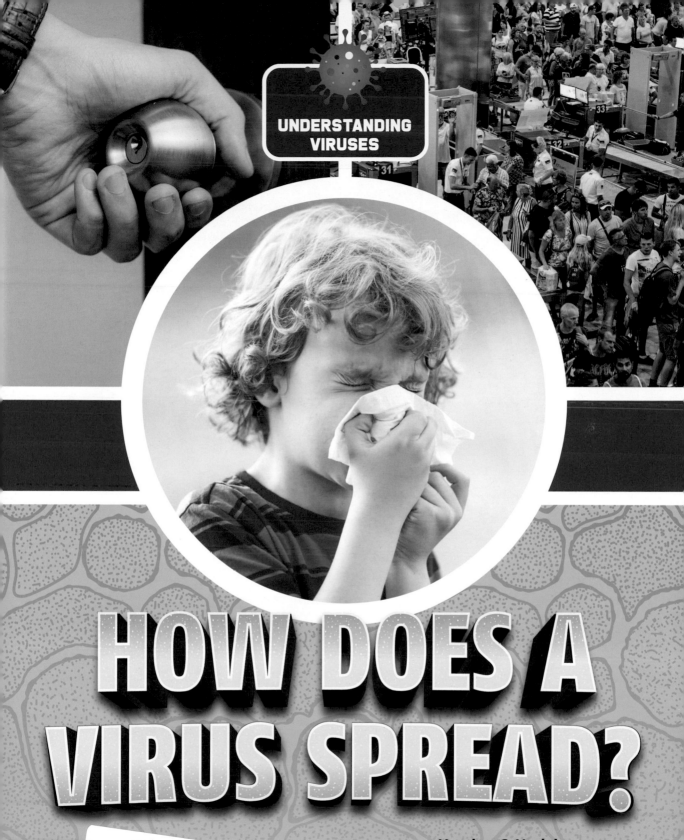

UNDERSTANDING VIRUSES

HOW DOES A VIRUS SPREAD?

Heather C. Hudak

books.com

Step 1
Go to **www.av2books.com**

Step 2
Enter this unique code

WHBCPNWLF

Step 3
Explore your interactive eBook!

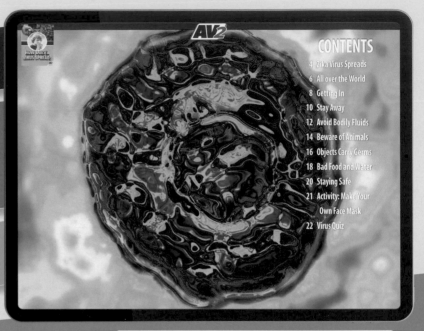

HOW DOES A VIRUS SPREAD

CONTENTS

AV2 is optimized for use on any device

Your interactive eBook comes with...

Contents
Browse a live contents page to easily navigate through resources

Audio
Listen to sections of the book read aloud

Videos
Watch informative video clips

Weblinks
Gain additional information for research

Try This!
Complete activities and hands-on experiments

Key Words
Study vocabulary, and complete a matching word activity

Quizzes
Test your knowledge

Slideshows
View images and captions

... and much, much more!

HOW DOES A VIRUS SPREAD?

CONTENTS

Zika Virus Spreads

Between 2013 and 2014, French Polynesia faced a Zika virus outbreak. About 30,000 people were **infected**. Before the outbreak, Zika was very rare. The virus mainly spreads to humans through mosquito bites and **bodily fluids**. Most people get better in a few days. However, pregnant women can pass Zika on to their unborn babies. Some of the babies are born with **birth defects**. There is no cure for Zika.

The virus made its way to the Americas in 2015. Zika struck Brazil first. It likely arrived with a person who had traveled from French Polynesia. Then, it quickly spread to other countries in South America and the Caribbean. Something had to be done to stop the spread. Governments taught people how to protect themselves. They put plans in place to reduce mosquito breeding grounds. In 2016, Zika cases in the Americas began to drop.

French Polynesia was heavily impacted by the 2013–2014 Zika outbreak. About 10 percent of its population contracted the virus.

FAST FACT

By December 2016, there were more than 532,000 Zika cases in 48 countries and territories in the Americas. There were 2,439 birth defects in 22 countries and territories due to Zika.

All over the World

Viruses are very tiny germs. They are so small that billions of them could live on the head of a pin. Different types of viruses may get inside different kinds of **organisms** and make them sick. People, plants, and animals can all act as hosts for viruses. A virus may attack different organs and tissues in the human body once it gets inside. It can be deadly if the body cannot fight it off.

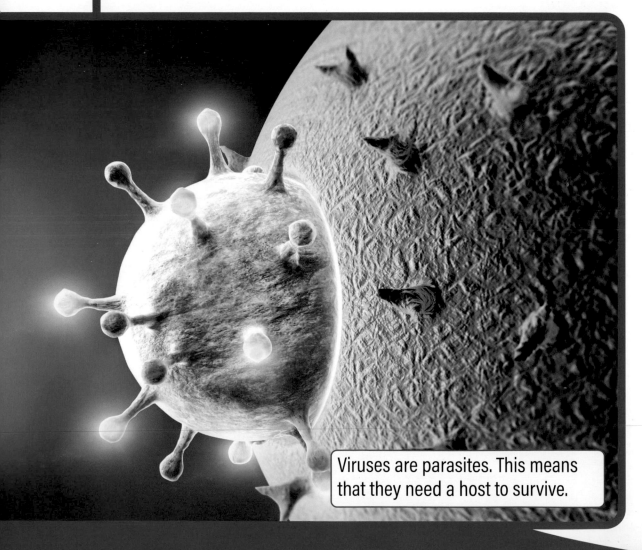

Viruses are parasites. This means that they need a host to survive.

Understanding Viruses

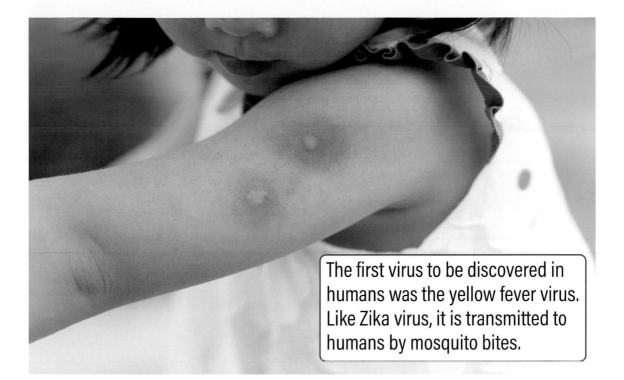

The first virus to be discovered in humans was the yellow fever virus. Like Zika virus, it is transmitted to humans by mosquito bites.

To date, only a few hundred viruses are known to infect humans. However, new viruses are discovered each year. The common cold, chickenpox, and the flu are caused by viruses that spread quickly and easily. These infections usually clear up on their own after a few days. Other viruses can make people very sick. HIV and hepatitis can be very harmful and last a long time. They can even be deadly.

Bacteria or Viruses?

Like viruses, bacteria are tiny germs. However, they do not need a host to survive. Bacteria are organisms with only one cell. They can live almost anywhere on Earth.

Getting In

A virus has two main parts. The first is nucleic acid. This is a set of instructions that tells the virus what to do once it gets inside a host. The second is a coat of protein called the capsid. The capsid acts like a shell to protect the nucleic acid. It has feelers that stick out from the shell. They look for the right type of cell to infect. Then, they trick the cell into thinking that the virus is a type of nutrient. The cell pulls the virus inside. Some viruses have a third layer. It is called the **lipid** envelope. Like the capsid, the lipid envelope helps protect the virus so that the virus can spread.

Once inside a host, viruses take over the host's cells and use them to make copies of themselves. One virus can make millions of other viruses inside a host. Once infected, the host carries the virus and spreads it to others.

People who catch the flu virus can be contagious even before their symptoms begin.

Some scientists do not consider viruses to be alive. This is because they do not grow, move, or use energy.

How a Virus Works

This graphic shows what happens when a virus gets inside a cell.

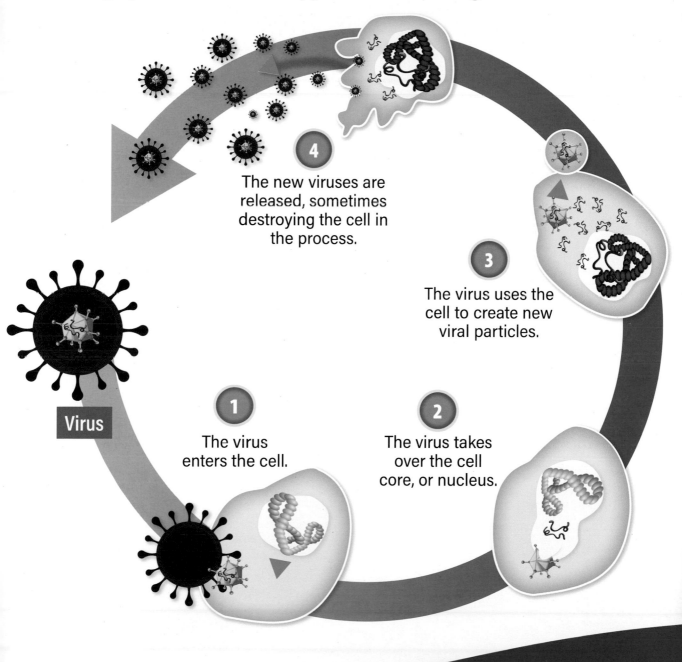

Virus

4 The new viruses are released, sometimes destroying the cell in the process.

3 The virus uses the cell to create new viral particles.

1 The virus enters the cell.

2 The virus takes over the cell core, or nucleus.

Stay Away

O ne of the main ways that viruses spread is from person to person. Viruses come out in tiny droplets when a sick person talks, coughs, or sneezes. The droplets then move through the air. Most travel up to 6 feet (1.8 meters). They get inside other people's noses and mouths when they breathe. The droplets can also land in a person's eyes. Many diseases, such as the flu, the common cold, rubella, and **COVID-19** spread this way.

To be effective, a face mask should never be touched with dirty hands. It should be removed from the back without touching the part that covers the mouth and nose.

Even if people do not feel sick, they may carry a virus. Some people never show symptoms. Others may not show signs of illness for many days after they get the virus. However, they can still spread it to others. People should always cough and sneeze into the crook of their arm. This helps stop droplets from getting into the air. A sick person can wear a mask over his or her mouth and nose to avoid spreading droplets.

Scientists think that the average person who catches the COVID-19 virus might transmit it to up to six people.

Do Not Touch

Some viruses spread when the skin of an infected person touches another person's skin. Viruses can also spread through contact with **mucous membranes**. Cold sores, warts, and chickenpox are caused by viruses that spread in this way.

Avoid Bodily Fluids

A virus can spread through contact with the bodily fluids of an infected person. Hepatitis and HIV spread this way. The body tissues and organs of an infected person may also carry viruses. Bodily fluids can only infect a person if they have a way in. Health workers use needles to take blood or give vaccines. The needles get bodily fluids on them. Workers must be careful not to get pricked by an infected needle.

Hepatitis mainly affects the liver. The liver is an organ that cleans the blood from toxins and produces a substance called bile that helps digest food.

Covering a fresh cut helps keep it clean and free from dirt and germs.

People can come in contact with bodily fluids through fresh cuts and cracks in the skin. Bodily fluids may also splash into a person's eyes, nose, or mouth. They can pass from a mother to an unborn child as well. Some viruses live in dried blood for many days. People should never use an infected person's razor, nail clippers, or tweezers.

FAST FACT

Syringe needles were invented in 1853. Single-use plastic syringes were developed almost one century later. Until then, syringes and their needles were **sterilized** and reused for different patients.

Beware of Animals

Some viruses carried by animals can be passed to people. The diseases caused by these viruses are called zoonotic diseases. Often, the virus does not cause harm to the animal. Sick animals may even seem healthy. However, some zoonotic diseases can make people very ill. For instance, some bats carry rabies or the Ebola virus.

People can get zoonotic diseases by petting or touching an infected animal. Viruses can also pass through bites, scratches, and droplets that come from an infected animal. People should always wash their hands with warm, soapy water after being near an animal. This helps stop the spread of viruses. Eating food sourced from an infected animal might also be a risk. Meat, dairy, and seafood can carry viruses.

Some viruses are carried by insects, such as mosquitoes, ticks, and sand flies.

Zoonotic Diseases around the World

This map shows where some important zoonotic diseases caused by viruses were first discovered.

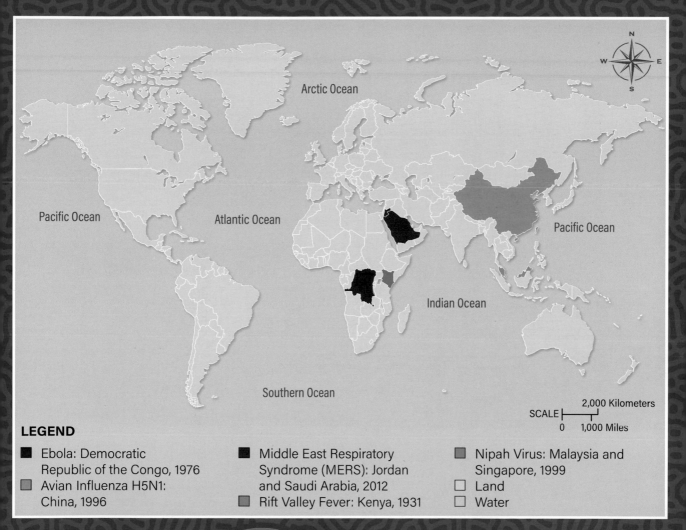

Arctic Ocean

Pacific Ocean

Atlantic Ocean

Pacific Ocean

Indian Ocean

Southern Ocean

SCALE

2,000 Kilometers

0   1,000 Miles

LEGEND

■ Ebola: Democratic Republic of the Congo, 1976

■ Avian Influenza H5N1: China, 1996

■ Middle East Respiratory Syndrome (MERS): Jordan and Saudi Arabia, 2012

■ Rift Valley Fever: Kenya, 1931

■ Nipah Virus: Malaysia and Singapore, 1999

☐ Land

☐ Water

Many viruses are carried by *Aedes* mosquitoes. These mosquitoes have black and white marks on their bodies and legs.

Objects Carry Germs

Droplets that come from an infected person spread through the air. Then, they land on counters, desks, and other surfaces. People can get the virus if they touch the objects and then touch their eyes, nose, or mouth. Viruses cannot live without a host for very long. Most live only a few hours. Some live a few days. They can infect a person during this time. The flu virus can live for at least 24 hours on plastic and metal.

Sick people sometimes cough or sneeze into their hands. They may not wash their hands right away. They might open a door, touch a faucet, or use a remote control before they wash their hands. The virus can spread to others through these objects, too. Pink eye, the flu, and measles are a few examples of viruses that spread through contact with infected objects.

Cell phones are some of the dirtiest objects in our everyday lives. Experts recommend cleaning them at least twice a day.

Keep It Clean

Most homes are filled with objects that carry germs. People touch these objects all the time without thinking about how dirty they are. Here are some tips to improve hygiene at home.

Regularly clean objects and surfaces that are often touched, such as TV remotes, doorknobs, fridge and cabinet doors, countertops, and taps.

If a surface might be **contaminated**, clean it using special products that kill germs.

When cleaning, use disposable wipes, paper towels, or reusable cloths that can be thoroughly washed.

When in the house, take off your shoes. Do not wear clothes that have been worn outside.

Wash your hands regularly before and after touching objects around the house. Every person in the house should have his or her own hand towel.

Bad Food and Water

People can get viruses from eating infected foods. Some foods are contaminated when they are made. People who work in restaurants or factories may be carrying a virus. They spread the virus to the food when they prepare it. People who touch fruits or vegetables in stores may also have a virus. The virus can then infect people who eat the foods.

Some parts of the world do not have proper **sewage** treatment. These places do not have the tools to remove waste from water. Viruses from the waste may then get into drinking water. They can make people sick. Viruses may also get into the water farmers use to water their crops. Crops can then become infected.

Raw meat, dairy products, fish, eggs, and **poultry** can all carry viruses. People can get viruses from eating the meat or organs of an infected animal. Meat should be well cooked to help kill any viruses.

Water must be boiled if there is no clean source. People can also drink bottled water instead.

Fruits and vegetables should be washed well before eating or cutting them.

Contaminated Foods

This graph shows the foods that made people sick between 2009 and 2016, according to the U.S. Center for Disease Control and Prevention (CDC).

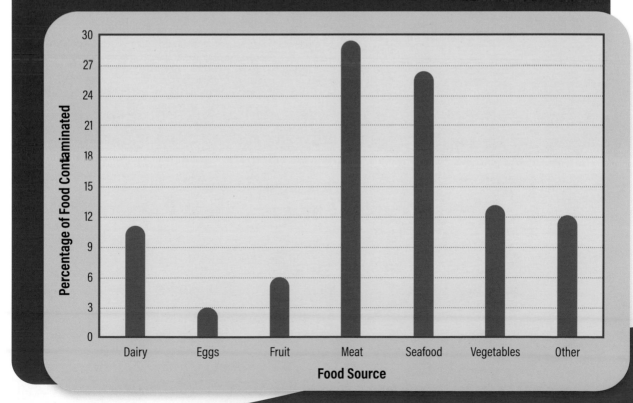

Staying Safe

Vaccines are the best way to protect against viruses. They involve giving a person a small amount of a virus. This helps the body build up **immunity**.

People should use a tissue to cover their mouth and nose when they sneeze or cough. They should then throw out the used tissue and wash their hands. People can use the bend of their arm or upper arm if they do not have a tissue. These body parts rarely come in contact with objects or the people. Washing the hands often can help stop viruses from spreading. People should also be sure to scrub their nails, thumbs, and between each fingers.

People who feel sick should avoid contact with others. They should stay home from work or school. They should not share food, drinks, or dishes with anyone. It is best to clean any objects the sick person may have touched. **Disinfectants** help kill any germs.

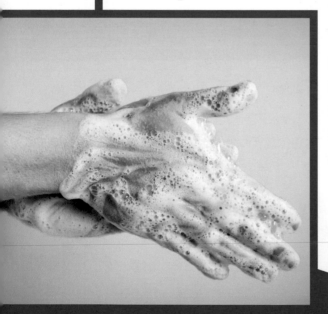

People should wash their hands for at least 20 seconds. This ensures that most germs are removed.

Make Your Own Face Mask

Experts recommend the use of face masks during an outbreak of a virus. Masks can help reduce the spread of the virus. This is because people who wear masks are less likely to spread infected droplets. While medical mask supplies should be reserved for health workers, people can wear nonmedical masks. Here is how you can make one:

What You Need
- A piece of tightly woven fabric, such as cotton or linen
- Scissors
- Rubber bands or hair ties

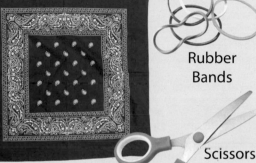

Rubber Bands

Fabric

Scissors

What to Do
1. Disinfect your workspace and wash your hands.
2. With the help of an adult, cut your piece of fabric to be approximately 20 by 20 inches (51 by 51 centimeters). You can use an old T-shirt for the fabric. A bandana might also work.
3. Fold your piece of fabric in half.
4. Fold the top part of your piece of fabric down and the bottom part up. You will now have a thin rectangle.
5. Slide your rubber bands or hair ties on both ends of the rectangle. They should be about 6 inches (15 cm) apart.
6. Fold the sides of the rectangle to the middle and tuck them.
7. Your mask is ready to wear. Remember to change your mask often and wash it thoroughly after every use.

VIRUS QUIZ

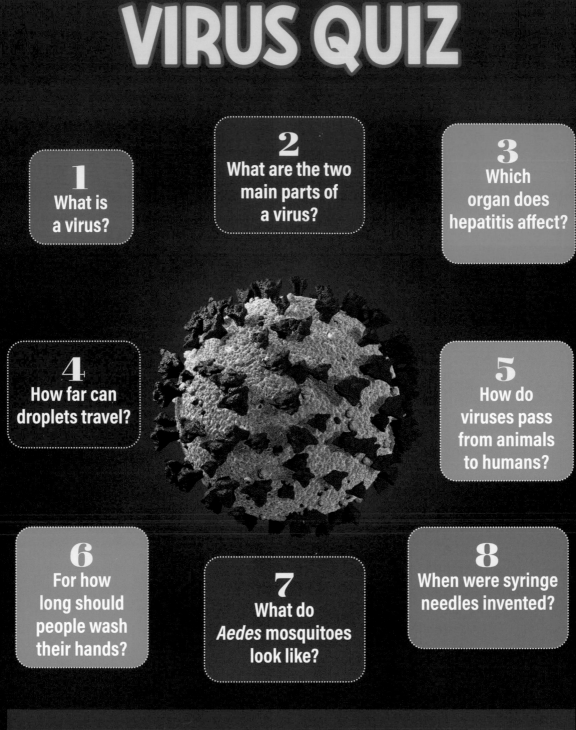

1
What is
a virus?

2
What are the two
main parts of
a virus?

3
Which
organ does
hepatitis affect?

4
How far can
droplets travel?

5
How do
viruses pass
from animals
to humans?

6
For how
long should
people wash
their hands?

7
What do
Aedes mosquitoes
look like?

8
When were syringe
needles invented?

ANSWERS
1. A tiny germ 2. Nucleic acid and capsid 3. The liver 4. Up to 6 feet (1.8 m) 5. Humans might catch a virus by petting or touching an infected animal, if bitten or scratched by an infected animal, or when coming in contact with infected droplets from an animal 6. For at least 20 seconds 7. They have black and white marks on their bodies and legs 8. 1853

Key Words

birth defects: minor or severe problems that happen when a baby is still forming inside its mother

bodily fluids: fluids that come from the body, such as blood or saliva

contaminated: made impure or harmful

COVID-19: a viral disease that can cause cough, fever, and trouble breathing, among other symptoms

disinfectants: chemicals that destroy harmful germs

immunity: the ability to ward off infections

infected: came in contact with a virus that then entered the system

lipid: a substance that does not break down in water

mucous membranes: protective layers that line many parts of the body and help keep out dust and germs

organisms: living beings, such as plants, animals, or single-celled life-forms

poultry: birds that are domesticated for eggs and meat

sewage: waste that comes from a community and is found in sewers

sterilized: made free from germs

Index

AV2

Get the best of both worlds.

AV2 bridges the gap between print and digital.

The expandable resources toolbar enables quick access to content including **videos**, **audio**, **activities**, **weblinks**, **slideshows**, **quizzes**, and **key words**.

Animated videos make static images come alive.

Resource icons on each page help readers to further **explore key concepts**.

Published by AV2
14 Penn Plaza, 9th Floor
New York, NY 10122
Website: www.av2books.com

Library of Congress Control Number: 2020940985

ISBN 978-1-7911-3258-3 (hardcover)
ISBN 978-1-7911-3259-0 (softcover)
ISBN 978-1-7911-3260-6 (multi-user eBook)
ISBN 978-1-7911-3261-3 (single-user eBook)

Printed in Guangzhou, China
1 2 3 4 5 6 7 8 9 0 24 23 22 21 20

072020
101119

Project Coordinator: Sara Cucini
Designer: Terry Paulhus